Buffalo Circles

Conjuring the Buffalo Way

Copyright © 2020 – **Jimmy Santiago Baca**

All rights reserved. No portion of this publication may be reproduced, stored in a retrieval system, or transmitted in any form or by any other means, electronic, mechanical, photocopying, or recording without prior permission of the individual authors unless such copying is expressly permitted by federal copyright law. Address inquiries in permissions to: Swimming with Elephants Publications: swimmingwithelephants.com
swimwithelephants@gmail.com

Cover art, copyright 2020© **Michael Glenn Bish**
– all rights reserved.

About Buffalo Circles

Buffalo Circles are community forums where people explore ways to include their love for wildlife and learn from it. With a little imagination, Buffalo Circles have the ability to teach us to see through Earth's eyes and through the eyes of her most valued creations.

The buffalo have taught us much about resilience and strength throughout their tumultuous history, now they are teaching us how to forgive, nurture, and endure—to come back from being driven to near extinction by our gluttonous attitudes, to warn us to balance our lives, to respect our all mutual brothers and sisters—whether winged, hoofed, or finned.

The goal of this collection is an invitation for people to create Buffalo Circles in their own communities in order to provide a common place for interaction and awareness. People everywhere have the ability to create a local Buffalo Circle which can become a significant and vital part of their lives. Buffalo Circles may consist of weekly or monthly engagements, where people exchange ideas and experiences, as well as learn and contribute to the ideas of others. Through Buffalo Circles, we can teach and inspire others through our paintings, poems, stories, and dances, and by doing so we give our lives a deeper, meaningful experience living within the circle of wildlife.

Buffalo Circles can provide community and growth, and most importantly, each can be unique to fit the needs of our current lives. As few as two or three people may comprise a Buffalo Circle and it can grow to accommodate an entire society. Buffalo Circles are a model that fits our lives today by allowing us to share feelings, be relevant, and be aware.

With so many of us looking for ways to live with integrity and conviction—Buffalo Circles have the potential to make us as momentous as the beautiful beasts for which they are named.

Jimmy Santiago Baca
November 2020

Wildlife Conservation Society (WCS) Rocky Mountain Program

The Rocky Mountains are the beating heart of wild North America. Buffalo, jaguar, wolverine, grizzly bear, bighorn, and beaver roam these wild and working lands. The diversity of cultures and well-stewarded Indigenous and private lands in the region mirror the Rockies' ecological richness. WCS's vision is to *Rewild the Rockies* by braiding science and cultural knowledge, policy, strategic partnerships, and civic engagement and movement building. We recognize the need to co-create a novel, transformational conservation paradigm that dissolves the barriers that divide us from the natural world and ourselves, and breathes life into the principles of justice, equity, diversity, and inclusion.

Learn more: Rockies.wcs.org.

Contents

Buffalo Rain 1
    Jimmy Santiago Baca

a Native Irish woman writes a poem about the buffalo 7
    Pamela Mary Brown

the revolution is *one* 9
    Pamela Mary Brown

Buffalo at a Rest Stop 13
    Matthew Cuban Hernandez

Buffalo Soldier 16
    Anna Martinez

Serás tu, Capitán 20
    Anna Martinez

this is how we pray 25
    Cristina Lee Mormorunni

Living Between the Worlds: The Seen & the Unseen 29
    Cristina Lee Mormorunni

Buffalo 33
    Jorge Nunez & Chris Henrikson

Elote Man **35**
  Jorge Nunez

A Yearning for Balance and Truth in My Own Heart and Spirit **38**
  Carey Powers

Buffalo on a Plain Somewhere in North America **44**
  Garland Thompson, Jr.

Buffalo Rain

Jimmy Santiago Baca

Strong rain—big, hard masculine drops
smack the canyon forest pines. I hear
a black-nostril'd heave, sigh over the fields.

In the meadow beyond my cabin
Buffalo rain grazes in the morning mist,
 nibbles withered grasstips,
wrenches at the day-moon
hanging in dew on twigs—

The Buffalos clomp
 over the once-new 2x4's,
(I was going to use building the dog pen,
blackened by a year's weather in the weeds.)

A Hopi friend tells me
gnarly white ginger roots
I'm planting this year,
 are buffalo-spirit hooves,
that dig at earth until it thaws through
 to release
barrel-chested healthy nubs.

I think of this as I watch
Buffalo rain
in the same meadows
kids from the village

brought O'Keeffe to,
where she found the colors she dreamed of
 for her painting.

The children told her what each flower was,
its medicinal and ceremonial use,
how the petals sweep
the blue from sky and save the sky in roots/petals—
(imagine saving sky . . . the way you do pennies in a jar!),
they taught her Chicano/Indio names,
instructed her in the ways of grandmothers
distilling pigments from blossoms and stems.
Without them, there'd be no O'Keeffe paintings
as we know them.

In the 1850s the village was a trading post
where Hopis, Utes, Apaches, Comancheros
Kiowa, Dene, a few Crow and Lakota
traded captives and horses,
a village (not a pueblo), Mexicans
and Indios married, and today we have more tribes
living side by side than anywhere else.

They say O'Keeffe painted the cliffs
behind my cabin and sold the canyon series
for millions to the Kemper museum in Kansas City.
Made her famous and wealthy,
while the villagers were given oranges
and thought they were eating tiny suns.

The same cliffs

I pray to each morning, same cliffs my ancestors
appear each night in ghost form, dancing and praying.
I see them when I go hiking,
two-hundred-year-old young couples sitting in boulders
scooped out by centuries of rain, kissing.
Meet my uncle spirit hunters in other boulders

carved out with stone chisels,
sit in and wait for elk or turkey to come by.
In some boulders chiseled by wind,
young warriors perch as lookouts
for raiding parties.
Some rocks have been whittled smooth
to divert rainwater to gather in pools.

I visit these sacred places and pray, drink the water,
nod to my ancestors—tios, tias, abuelo/as y padres,
 see them as clearly as I do my hand.

I thank them for permitting me to be here.

Each morning I ask them for guidance.
Each morning I offer my heart to them.

Later, I catch the morning news,
where viral hornets are swarming cities—
                Nature, I think,
self-correcting what we haven't,
balancing people out of whack,
arrives to clean house.

Gives Mother Earth a reprieve from our greed.
Pollution decreases. Traffic lessens. Power Mongers
pause grunting at the trough—
no more maddening gotta-have gotta-do,
no more gluttonous consumption of oil,
no more guzzling consumers,
—not a nuclear bomb or White Dictator
that's come to destroy,
but a tiny invisible microscopic
    Leveler,
    Balancer—

we expected Brown People, Chicanos & Mexicans,
 we caged them, separated families, murdered them;
we imagined them wielding weapons—
   drugs, alcohol, bombs,
they warned us these would be the enemy
but an aerial corona star appears in the blood
to settle the books,
empty every commercial establishment,
 force humans to cower behind locked doors.

The enemy didn't come at us crossing borders,
swinging machetes and machine guns.
A benign emperor embracing us in groups and crowds,
merging into our breathing, in his glittering carriage, came.

Far from the closest person,
I've only spoken a few words to in thirty years,
in this womb of cliffs
silence is the language I speak,

suspends its mist over everything—

I stand on the porch
listening to the raindrops
tick the green galvanized roof.

Some leaves
didn't fall this winter,
clutter the boughs
still trying to clutch on to Spring,
to what they had,
to what they were, and their failure's
meaning of life
is to surrender—
nothing holds on to what it had,
to what it was.

Gust-clusters strong enough to shove me back,
hackle the crackly beige leaves,
make Bella (my Corso) turn
searching animal movement,
catching a whiff, she lunges tonguelong
growling after ancestral spirits that kindle the air,
tracking their glittering with sniffs
over boulders into the weeds,
dashing up a wildlife trail,
baptized by brush
sparkling rain over her.

I watch
and the silence whispers:

Do not hold on to what you had, Jimmy,
to who you were.
                Live light.

a Native Irish woman writes a poem about the buffalo

Pamela Mary Brown

I take my fingers and trace its spine
and imagine a mountain range
from Alaska to New Mexico

I see the Great Plains, a wilderness haven—
an obstinacy of buffalo
Henry Thoreau beard and belly beautiful

here under a gentian sky
who understands loss and endurance?
we whose cultures have been mocked and ridiculed

the eye discerning the Irish landscape
from the isle of Doagh to Skibbereen
Doolough to Drogheda on the Boyne

our famine walls—diseased workhouses
mass graves on roads-sides
ghost villages—white crosses

—*an Gorta Mor*— the great hurt
the genocide of tribe and clan
betrayal and dispossession

who revises the lies of our stolen history?

the voice of the Gaels
in need of *Seanchaí* and Shaman

we gather the starving millions
into our native arms
they are our poems and our songs

the *Book of Invasions*: conquered
yet unbroken
and memory is our offering—ever sacred

where on the Hill of Uisneach
the *Bealtaine* fires are blazing
the kindling of the sun

the re-birth of the land after winter
the symbols of hope in our hands
the buffalo story—renewal and survival

I take my fingers and trace its spine
and hold our truths as indestructible
our spirits faithful—untamed and untameable.

the revolution is *one*

Pamela Mary Brown

I have been waiting on the revolution
ever since I first heard the word revolution
I have been waiting on the revolution
ever since that word first dripped
freedom from my tongue
I have been waiting on the promised dawn
the echoes of chanting cries that
pulse the hearts of nations
an alleluia morning of transformation
a daybreak of reform
a sunrise of rebellion
a genesis of change
a collective truth protesting to an off beat
that is a new beat
not a down beat
or a beat down beat
but a beat the system beat
beat the fat cats beat

fat cat bankers
fat cat constructers
fat cat politicians
fat cat war criminals—

fat cats, colluding to crippling with capitalist policies
fat cats, crony greed white collar fraudsters

fat cats, nourishing discrimination
fat cats, the puppet masters of inequality
fat cats who have ensured that there are now more
human slaves on this planet
than at any other time in our history

I have been waiting on the revolution
without really understanding what
the revolution means—

the revolution is not a commodity
it cannot be bought or sold by parasitic prosperity
blind eye infallibility
someone else's doorstep negating responsibility—

the revolution is *one*
one person willing to make a move
stand up or sit down or walk away from any illusion
the revolution is one person leaving
a domestic violent relationship
one student marching for civil rights
one housewife speaking out against human rights
violations

the revolution is my brother
who never lets his pen rest
one letter to the government about education cuts
one voice challenging financial corruption
one worker joining a union

the revolution is one doctor driven by
the compassion to heal
one teacher honouring their vocation
one woman standing up to the manufacturers of
weapons of mass destruction—

the revolution is chipping away at convention
the revolution is food, clothes and shelter
the revolution is one awakening tired of giving in
or not giving out, or giving up, or not giving a damn or
always giving an inch—

the revolution is one victim speaking
the name of the perpetrators of child abuse
the revolution is a priest who can climb
down from his pulpit
and accept the collective responsibility
of cover ups and collusion—

the revolution is my sister
who will not be bullied or let her children
be bullied by better left unspoken
one father speaking out about homophobic
hate crime against his son
one ambulance with medical aid
reaching its destination—

the revolution is one pebble in the pond
one flutter of the butterfly wings

one mind opening
one breath worth breathing

one fat cat retreating
one fat cat tossing and turning
one fat cat backtracking
one fat cat's resignation

the revolution is not once upon a time
or once in a blue moon kingdom
the revolution is not waiting
the revolution is some-*one*
the revolution is any-*one*
the revolution is every-*one*
the revolution is one by one by one by one by one…

Buffalo at a Rest Stop

Matthew Cuban Hernandez

In 2009 I was 21 years old,
a brown boy
with good health
and purpose.
I wanted to travel, share my poetry with anyone
who would listen.
I spent most of the year alone.
Driving more hours than money made.
This had to be love?
Had to be land ancestors farmed and resources
for shelter. Had to be a lesson
waiting to be learned. Sometimes in the blackness of
night I would only see stars,
no road, no cars, just stars.
I would imagine the spirits
watched those same stars flicker
then fade. I would
find myself searching for reasons
to slow or sit still. Trying to hold tight
the rubber band of time.

Sleep in most places was a rest stop.
Small communities that felt like home
for a few hours. Sometimes there was information
about the land you were driving across.
A faded board ignored by all who drifted
through oasis.
After long enough I felt like that board.
Something only seen at the corners of eyes.
Something thriving and inspirational
then nearly snuffed out.
Somewhere between a sold out show and stealing food,
I found a gift shop in the desert.
And though the small store was beautiful
decorated with stories only this town could tell,
it was the lumbering mass of fur
and horns that pulled my attention.
At the time
I had never seen a buffalo.
Only in books
or songs about home.
But here it was
hulking in front of me
like a shadow I've been chasing

since I learned to write
my name.
He was just standing there.
Half covered in mud.
Half waiting, for something
my life would never teach me.
We met eye to eye.
As if to say,
"You finally made it all the way out here huh."
To face the storm in front of you
instead of sheltering. To survive
in spite of everything that wants you extinct.
So much of life felt like a dream.
Felt like challenging life
Like standing strong while covered in mud,
and still holding regal on my dignity.

Buffalo Soldier

(for Ahjani)

Anna Martinez

Meanwhile
in daylight on the dark side
in a world full of weeping yet so full of song
where every footfall's a prayer
appears
approaches in white
adobe girl floated down from stars

barefooted across the plains
snakes and wolves at her feet
She of so many names and yet
anybody's baby

indigenous girl
White Buffalo
thoughts dance behind her flashing eyes
where few could look and those who dared
saw pools of perfect blackness
themselves
as they really were
naked and revealed

when she finally spoke
her voice

the song of waters upon rocks
cracked
choked
oozing black serpent spew
from being slit gullet to womb
so deep as to dislodge the electric charge of
her beating heart
millions of years to bury what was best left buried
a million gallons of pick your poison
slow killing all it touches

young mothers suckle babies
with milk of breasts fed from
wells and creeks where their cattle and sheep drink
where since the beginning has leached and leaked
A MILLION GALLONS OF
RADIOACTIVE WASTE
a million gallons of oil they will actually claim
a million buffalo slaughtered for show
a million smallpox blankets for the cold
a million gallons of whiskey for your vote
a million voters purged from the rolls
a million children ripped from their homes and their
tongues from their throats
a million daughters right now being
bought raped and sold
a million more murdered and missing and
erasure of
their trail of tears

leaves them cold

a million unmarked graves
planted in fields of unrequited hate
where she does not even count
enough to be counted

oh but she counts
is all that counts
and she is counting down and

oh when the true west wind blows
her name remembered
lonely drum songs burnt across the plain
beware the rain that comes
once his lament has been sung

Oh girl every time I see you
you put a smile on my face
takes me to this beautiful place
oh how I wish that you were mine
I'd be happy all the time

you see
her friends are all warriors now
so take it slow
wait for them to ask you who you know
make no sudden moves
you know not the medicines they use

she'll stretch out her arms
palms facing the sun
know the direction from which her enemies come
binding
unbinding of her long blowing mane
whirling cloud of wind hail lightening appears in her name
unfurled
unleashed
the wrath of the love of a million sons
no watershed safe
no artery escapes
you're best to hunker down
it's gonna be
hard
hard rain.

Serás tu, Capitán

> Supreme Chief of the
> Revolutionary Movement of the South

Anna Martinez

That night
Zapata washed my feet
handlebar whiskers scratch the itch between
my legs like myth
reflected in the moon on the mesa like
tongue
of silver sage reaching as
he rides and rides underneath the moon's watchful
breath
rides and rides all night in great quicksilver strides
calor de aliente, respiras caliente
wings of exhale lead the way
smell of earth and dirt disturbed into flight by those
four legs forged in steel like
hands carved from the dust that flies to the beat of the
earth

this land belongs to those who work it with their hands
mi campesino
where it was law that money ruled all
you took it back
gave it back
plowed fields and *acequias*

planted schools and *campesino* credit unions
self-ruling
communitarian
democracy
un pueblo unido
the politic of confidence
always incites betrayal

'the city is full of sidewalks' you say
'and I keep falling off them'

pay no mind to that
what with twenty thousand soldiers
you overthrew the capital *Capitán*
not in rape and plunder
but thirst and hunger
knocking door to door asking for food and water
trai'me ese hambre commandánte
y tu sed te injusticia
que te esperan mis botas
a pie, y sobre el llano te llama mi llanto
y te dibujare con mi canto
y seras tu, Zapata
quien eschucho tocandome en la mañanita

come to me
Supreme Chief of the
Revolutionary Movement of the South
fly home like falcon

roost in my mouth
yet to remain free
untethered
as we understand
the battle is left at the door

enter

on my knees
I will remove your boots
and the shame of your tears
as you overthrew the capital
so you do now with me
here
as has always been my wish
eye to eye
ojo a ojo
frente a frente
raíces enredandose
jamás seremos vencidos
never again to be defeated
smell of earth and death disturbed into flight by our
four legs forged in steel like
hands carved from the dust that
flies to the beat of the earth as
your eyes understand my fight and
your hands recover my lands
as promised a time of truth and justice
now rest

face buried in my chest
inhaling sweat and tears from my breast
lost in my blood
hint of copper on your lips
kiss me
I will finally find homeland
Atzlán
in the aura of your crown
magic from which others turn and run yet
I stand ground and call

oleme
in smoke of your body riddled with bullets
fired from every of their rifles
until emptied
escúchame
in the laughter of 50,000 pesos
besos de traidor
MATENLO
then in the footsteps of the burro
that carries you home to Cuautla
for only half the bounty
your body displayed
photographed as proof
of your non existence

so why did the one have to die
for you to arrive
as between the two

who is truth
as still your horse can be seen
prancing
galloping
bucking
reflecting silver underneath the sun
even as the time for talk is done
nothing now but await your hoof beat
you need but reach your arm for my leap
we'll raise dust from this place
silver tongued sages reaching
as you and I
finally
ride away.

this is how we pray

Cristina Lee Mormorunni

hooves heave earth,
beat out ancient rhythms
hide flinches, ears flick, horns toss, tail lifts
we race on broad warm backs from
a profane past into the unknown future
slicing through the impossibility of the present.

RECOGNITION.

hearts sing faster faster   faster and faster
in time to something long gone   still present   so
large
calling it home.

lips sing gratitude,
pour love-devotion into yielding wetness,
thick gray tails wag
low   and   slow,
lips curling.

RELATION.

we blow warm animal breaths   blow sky
   apart
in unison.

antlers caress the veil between the worlds, coax open the
hard truth of the sacred,
brush our cheeks with velvet kisses,
tickle hardened hearts until they smile.

RESPECT.

we slash clouds into thin blue vapors,
leave holes the color of the air at midnight
now you see me, now you
don't
       we roar,
ruthless   ferocious
       mourning   together.
there is nothing to lose when all has been taken.

RECIPROCITY.

fur shapeshifts into feather,
steamy wings beat through water-laden air

thunder lightening
piercing shafts of blinding color.
pale fur belly returns back to the earth,
       opened   falling
until feral claws find purchase
in moist timbered dirt,
stalk shadow, return light
carried tenderly on bird tongue.

REWILDED.

your moon-eye revolves around my sun-eye,
alchemy of fire   bound to wind and water and
earth   the four directions   in
wholeness.

starless hump you carry the planets,
glitter with the wisdom of a thousand raindrops,
silver light fills your eyes and I know why I am here.

REMATRIATION.

we bind wisdom to inky wingtips with ancestral webs,
load weighty truths on wide withers, carry them
to souls scorched by greed   self-loathing   and
fear.

we watch the sacred burn
watch it smolder smoke   and seethe.

"Fly," you say.
"Soar," you say.
"Run, you say.
"Quickly now," you scream.

paws hooves wings tails   pound   land
water air,
horns tear sky and

beaks open in a silent scream as the winged fall to the burning earth
    sacrifice
        stillness
    silent song
we choke on jagged hope,
the words cut our throat, singe our tongues, sting our eyes

    but this is how we pray.

        RECONCILIATION.

Living Between the Worlds: The Seen & the Unseen

Cristina Lee Mormorunni

> For the winged ones,
> the horned ones,
> the hooved ones
> —for all the Blessed Beings.

Sky clotted white and peach,
streaked with veins of icy-blue.
Air smells of buckled metal,
burnt rubber,
smoldering steel.

Nostrils flare, acrid.
Eyes sting, salt.
I love you while you die.

Tangle of elegant limbs. Fine ebony hooves.
Dream blanket of small pale stars cooling.

Tiny tail flicking fast   slowing slower still
quietening.

Pool of red froth shimmers, bringing
tired oiled asphalt alive.

Sinew, flesh, bone.
Glisten in the fading light.
I love you while you die.

Smashed   splintered scream
       bursts from miniature muzzle,
a black as dark as the deepest night.

The response
travels the distance
across the four lanes of hurtling steel at the speed of the most pained light.
Severs winter's steel armor.

What follows is a quiet so soft, so permanent

a sound that shears the frozen world,
forever.

I cradle felted pelt.
Caress flawless forehead.
Fear flares   an inconsequential protest.
Ears quiver, eyes clutch mine.

She murmurs, What are you?

I open arms wide. Lean towards perfect petal ear.
Whisper:

I guard the invisible door between the worlds.
You are safe.
Follow me.
Cross over.

Air smells of brine and ozone.
Far shore shimmers.
The call of the luminous Unseen World insistent now.

Breath warbles   rasps.
Foreheads touch,
and we share   one last warm breath.

Glimmer fades.
Eyes grow dull like those diorama animals in the
Steinhart Aquarium
that terrified   that froze my small
child heart,
        but
        prepared me for this,
        trained me for this,
        the brutal smallness of this,

                                        infinite

moment.
I love you while you die.

The Seen World
sinks milky teeth into tender flesh,

      rips, tears, slashes,
apart the Unseen World.

Numb. Greedy
in the freezing rain of
Separation.
Alienation.
Domination.

There is no pain,
No smell.
No color.
No sound.
As the Blessed Being takes her last breath.

I love you while you die.

Buffalo

Jorge Nunez & Chris Henrikson

I've been buffalo'd
Banged out
Hit up
Left to die
On concrete plains
A 15-year-old calf
Herded into a cage
With other strays
Twice my age
Shoulder to shoulder
Tattoo'd rage
Then released
Almost deceased
To find my way back
To where my people's bones
Lie broken and buried or
Bleached by blinding sunlight

It is time to reunite
On sacred ground
Where
We can bear the storms of Winter
And words designed to divide
And not be divided
We stand together
Facing the winds of change

Wild and uncontained
Outcasts from ancient herds
Circling the center pole
Again

We are the thunder
Of bassline and rhyme
Beneath steel-toed feet
And blood-stained streets
The rumble of a new day
Following the old ways home
A pipe and a prayer
An Eagle feather
Fresh air
Blowing in
From beyond cell block
And dope spot
To teach us how to breathe
Our bodies back
Into being
Freeing
What was once
Forgotten
From the earth.

Elote Man

Jorge Nunez

My three brothers, mother and I
Walked the streets of South LA
Pushed a shopping cart full of corn cobs
Yelling *"Elotes! Elotes!"*
Trying to get people to buy
To keep the sky from falling on our family
To make ends meet
A dent in our debt
One corn cob at a time
I remember it was my mom's last twenty dollars
She had to find a way to flip it to buy food for us all
We sold out that day, celebrating what we ate
I sold out another way
Robbing *elote* man after *elote* man
on my block and beyond
They saw me coming
They hid their money
Have you ever seen a grown man cry?
When I got to him
He´d already been taxed

And was empty-handed
Afraid for his life
Or the lives of the kids he'd fail to feed
Or the life of the wife he might not see
Because of me
Paperless like him
Feeling superior to my own kin
Because I spoke English
Because my skin was whiter
My pronunciation brighter
And that somehow gave me the right
I didn't understand that we both
came from the same land
The same earth
But the Universe, the Gods, call it what you will
Blessed me with the circumstance to see
Deported me seventeen years ago
And sometimes I still can't accept
Mexico is my home
But my thoughts are now brown and green like *nopales*
I stick my fingers in the dirt and
pull up potatoes and carrots
I pick broccoli

Plant kernels of the same corn I sold years ago as a child
Working under the same sun
On my own piece of land
I sweat the tears of many men
Struggle with the same fears
I am up before the sun rises and well after it sets
Arms stretched out to receive its blessing
Head held high because we are proud to be
Who we are
My people are noble
My people forgive
They embrace me
They welcome me home

A Yearning for Balance and Truth in My Own Heart and Spirit

Carey Powers

I sit in a snowstorm next to a herd of buffalo. All I can see is one buffalo's fur and the snow sweep into it. Each storm, each wind, each flurry, and still the buffalo will wait in the blizzard.

You could say, I waited there with them. Or I put my hand or ear to their fur.

The illusions are a gale. They tear at me and they have all my life. I feel my hands on fur and when I touch fur, the warmth keeps the frost from hardening.

The snow, it turns to water. Then I felt myself land feet first into a pool of water. The birds, I remember a woman I knew told a story that said the birds have memories. So I touch the fur again and we wait.

Yes, the birds have memories and I saw her as she waited by them. She is my grandmother. I saw her as she flew. In a story that someone told me was told many ways, the birds returned.

They had been killed, hunted, and nearly driven out. In the dream, or in the snow, she returned.

She sat there, I did and in the fire under her wrinkled hands were trenches in which seeds are planted.

In one version of the story, a long time ago, when I did not know I was human or yearning, it was another field, another animal.

The illusions, they and the living torment of mirrors, angles, sheaves, winters, scrambling, whining, stories, like the solidification of life, its' petrification, it's bruising and a kind of radiating, perfected stillness of illusion.

Corn grew from her, and in the wet frost, and daylight, and she shows me again the school and the children, and then I flew. And it was sunny on the wind.

And the other tears, those that washed the bird feet from landing in water, but show me the roundabouts of city streets from high above, retreat for fear, and why? They are my love as I crouch sowing seeds; they are all the half-formed, fragments of time that this love circled and released and bouldered through and waited within.

Silence.

Then the water glistens at the feet of all the plants.

Again, my grandmother and I sit by the fire in a snowstorm. The embers in the fire are a warm crackling spirit in my shoulders, they are not my bruises or my anger at illusions.

Then I swept the floor of a home, and the door, left wide open, quiet, outside which the voices of my children filled me also.

Then the gale came, a dark cloud, and it would like me to know it as prominent. I feel fighter jets in the hangar under my other shoulder. So she moves the coals.

The pages of a book are her hands when she weeps in winter.

A tear cannot be forced from the eye.

I talk about the school because it feels like my body; an imperfect blazing heart, built into and around and splitting those structures clean through their planks.

I lie awake in the night by her hand on my right arm and from her sprouts more plants. I see my friends and the stories that lived in everyone.

The gulls stepped in the water as the spray from a teal sea reached into the wisps of clouds. Where was that?

It is in the other arm, she said, and I turned over in the dark where the fire crackled so she could place her wrinkled hand on my left bicep.

From there I could see the land, its' every shape and tear, its grasses, its feet, its baskets, its clouds and its years. If she set sail strawberries in my waters, it was then.

If blueberries grew from me, it was then. And all the while I was thinking of people who told stories, and many-voiced stories.

The gull, for example, and I said, I see a gull on a rock on the mesa, and she said, of course you do. Then the warmth of the fire ran through me like a couch in the home of someone who has just left the door open, and who will return sometime in the afternoon with gifts from the land.

Cinnamon, or warm sun, or the bristles of the broom, and more sun warming my bones, and the heat moving through my bones as I lie down.

Then with great ease, the rivulets over the wetlands live their pulses.

It is spring; and dried meat hangs from a structure. That used to be an illusion my body tried to tell. That the wet silt carried hand prints, but only for a minute.

Again, my children are playing next to the meat and the linen lines.

Then I see myself on a rock over a meadow, above this home. A breeze comes, small yellow birds, and the telephone wires glisten with rainwater and sun, I grew happy with my love who sat beside me. The sky turns to rain.

We sat for as long as the fire was waiting to be lit on the land below.

We waited in the grasses. I saw roundabouts in the sky, wet, rainy dark songs rolling and being placed on the land.

I was warm there also. And with my coals, my grandmother comes with me through the meadows, and we laugh and laugh, on our knees, laughter so big, we double over, we lay, I lay in the grasses, in the grasses and burn; my bones will be fires tonight.

Buffalo on a Plain Somewhere in North America

Garland Thompson, Jr.

Sun slowly crawling over brown skin
like the brown covering the Buffalo.
Soft like a summer breeze.
As the clock ticks and clouds float by,
one can perceive the change
from shade to light.
Like a gentle but insistent wave
washing over you.

A Buffalo on a plain
somewhere in North America
glances up from its grazing,
feeling the heat on its skin.
Soon the big animal will move.
But for now, it stays in
the light as long as it can.
Enjoying the heat but knowing
there's a threshold it best not cross.

The Buffalo hears an airplane's
drone high in the distance
as it chews some prairie grass,
shifting its weight from side to side.

A prairie dog runs across the plain,
a jack rabbit too.

The big animal watches them both,
still in the sun.
Still hearing the plane passing by.
Does it wonder about that airplane?
Or does the Buffalo just eat, watch, and live.

Poets Biographies

Jimmy Santiago Baca's poetry titles include *Healing Earthquakes* (2001), *C-Train & 13 Mexicans* (2002), *Winter Poems Along the Rio Grande* (2004), and *Spring Poems Along the Rio Grande* (2007). In addition to the American Book Award, Baca has received a Pushcart Prize and the Hispanic Heritage Award for Literature. Baca has conducted writing workshops in prisons, libraries, and universities across the country for more than 30 years. In 2004, he launched Cedar Tree, a literary nonprofit designed to provide writing workshops, training, and outreach programs for at-risk youth, prisoners and former prisoners, and disadvantaged communities.

Pamela Mary Brown is *Writer-in-Residence* at HMP Magilligan, Editor of *Time In* magazine and Creative Writing Tutor-Assessor at the North West Regional College. Poet and author she has read her work in Ireland, UK and Holland; including Glastonbury, Manchester, Bristol, Dublin, Galway, Sligo, Cork, Electric Picnic, Flatlake Festival […]. Workshop and Creative Writing Facilitator at public venues, schools and institutions in Ireland/UK; she studied Community Drama at the University of Ulster; Media Studies at Foyle Arts Centre, Derry. She holds a BA (Hons) Degree in English Literature and Creative Writing and an MA in Creative Writing.Born in County Donegal, she has lived in Derry, in the North of Ireland, for more than 30 years.

Chris Henrikson is the founder of Street Poets Inc., a Los Angeles-based non-profit organization that harnesses the healing power of poetry and music to build community and inspire youth and young adults to write, rap and dream a new world into being – one rhyme at a time. Chris has 25 years of experience working in and around Los Angeles County's juvenile justice and educational systems, while facilitating youth initiation retreats and homecoming retreats for California State Prison parolees. He serves on the board of Wolf Connection and the Arts for Healing & Justice Network.

Matthew 'Cuban' Hernandez is a poet, emcee, speaker, and performance coach from Jacksonville, Florida. He has toured as far as Abu Dhabi and nearly every major city in the United States and Europe, performing, teaching and coaching poetry. A teaching artist for nearly ten years, Matthew has spent the last six years working in youth detention centers across Los Angeles County, currently serving as the Director of Camp Programming for Street Poets, Inc. In addition, he is a current Lead Teacher and Co-Founder of Spoken Literature Art Movement. Cuban has opened for artists such as Wu-Tang, performed for platforms such as BuzzFeed and NPR and even appeared on the award-winning television show, *Better Things*. Matthew is also a three time Southern Fried poetry slam champion and an award-winning poetry coach. Cuban's favorite activity is making people feel great; sometimes he does this through hip hop and poetry.

Anna C. Martinez is a local civil rights attorney, performance poet, mother and grandmother raised in Española, NM. First published in 2014 in anthologies *La Palabra: the Word is Woman*, and *Lowriting: Shots, Rides and Stories from the Chicano Soul* with artists such as Lalo Alcaraz, Gustavo Arellano and ABQ Poet Laureate Manuel Gonzalez, Anna is currently working on publishing her first book of poetry. Anna has held titles as ABQ XXX Haiku Champ, Chicano/a Slam Champ, and is on the board of directors for Burque Revolt Slam LLC and opens her home for free to traveling poets.

Cristina L. Mormorunni was born in San Francisco during the hey-day of the Summer of Love. Thus marked at birth and raised in a petri dish of passion and spitfire, she has spent the better part of her adult life working as a provocateur, an agent of change, a rebel, and a activist nomad. For the last twenty years, Cristina has devoted herself to conserving wild nature and transforming our world into a more just, beautiful, artful, compassionate, and healing place. She is currently honored to serve as the Regional Director for the Wildlife Conservation Society's Rocky Mountain Program (if you want to know more please check out:https://www.wcs.org/rockies-facethewind). While social change work comes with many perks, one of the most damaging occupational hazards of this line of work is a loss of the creative self and a gnawing misplacement of one's own artistic aspirations and power. When Cristina's creative muses started pounding on her door, finally splintering it, she applied to IAIA's

MFA in Creative Writing. Cristina has written and published work extensively as a part of her social change work, but it wasn't until shejoined the IAIA community that I she started calling herself a writer. She currently is working on a memoir about what it means to aspire to change the world—the benefits and costs—and how ultimately the greatest gift of this work is how it transforms you in the most unexpected ways in the process. The working title of her book is: *Anatomy of Betrayal: A Shattered Memoir*.

Jorge Nunez emigrated with his family to the United States from Mexico at the age of two, and was raised on the streets of Los Angeles. He fell into the gang life at a young age, and was on the fast-track to nowhere when he wrote his first poem while serving time in an L.A. County probation camp for boys. Poetry, and Street Poets, the non-profit organization that introduced him to that writing practice, became the lifeline that would see him through four years of state prison, followed by deportation to a country he barely knew. While incarcerated, Jorge was named the official Poet Laureate of California Men's Colony, where he did the majority of his time. One of the six original members of Street Poets' first poetry performance group as a youth in the late 90s, Jorge now serves as a guest poet and teaching artist in the organization's virtual workshops from his home in Tijuana, Mexico. He is a proud father of four with an A.A. degree in Mechatronic Engineering from Universidad Technologia de Tijuana, a passion for writing, and a deep hunger for life.

Carey Powers lives in Santa Fe, NM and is a graduate of the Institute of American Indian Arts' MFA Program in Poetry. She now works as a Teaching Assistant in the undergraduate department. Since graduating, she has been a Youth Outreach Fellow for the MFA and Continuing Education Department's Suicide Prevention Initiative, and participated in a graduate-led donation program for Navajo families during the pandemic. She is currently at work on a poetry collection.

Garland Thompson, Jr is an award-winning poet, actor, playwright, filmmaker, theater designer and producer. Garland got his start in Hollywood acting in the film *Madgame*, written by his father when he was five years old. After moving to NYC in his early teens, he began working in theater with some of the greatest companies ever including The Negro Ensemble Company, New Federal Theatre, Big Apple Circus, Public Theater, Manhattan Theatre Club, and American Place Theatre,. At 18, after coming to service the sound system, Garland was hired as the first official sound and lighting engineer for the Blue Note Jazz Club in NYC where he worked with seminal musicians such as Dizzy Gillespie, Carmen McCrae, Betty Carter, and Wayne Shorter. From 1997-2007 he produced the West Coast Championship Poetry Slam at the Henry Miller Library in Big Sur. He also brought the national recitation program **Poetry Out Loud** to Monterey County. He's worked with California Poets in the Schools, the Arts Council for Monterey County, and he was the 2007-08 Poet Laureate of Pacific Grove, CA. Until Covid hit he also produced and hosted the longest running Poetry Slam and Open Mic in Monterey County (17 years), known as the **Rubber Chicken Poetry Slam & Open Mic** at the East Village Coffee Lounge in downtown Monterey, CA. Currently he's the Executive Director of the Frank Silvera Writers' Workshop, a 47 year old theatre company in Brooklyn, NY, founded by his late father, Garland Lee Thompson, Sr., Actor/Producer Morgan Freeman, the late Journalist Clayton Riley, and the late Actor and Director, Billie Allen Henderson. In 2021 Garland's newest work, **Garland at 18: new book of poems**, will be published by Old Hat Press in Los Angeles.

Also available from
Swimming with Elephants Publications, LLC

Thalassophile
Abigayle Goldstein

the fall of a sparrow
Katrina K Guarascio

Shorn: apologies and vows
Benjamin Bormann

I've Been Cancelling Appointments with My Psychiatrist for Two Years Now
Sean William Dever

They Are All Me
Christina Dominque

Unease at Rest
Wil Gibson

bliss in die / unbinging the underglow
Bassam

from below / denied the light
Paulie Lipman

Language of Crossing
Liza Wolff-Francis

Find More Publications at:
swimmingwithelephants.com

www.ingramcontent.com/pod-product-compliance
Lightning Source LLC
Chambersburg PA
CBHW070451050426
42451CB00015B/3443